Peter Iljitsch Tschaikowsky
1840 – 1893

Die Jahreszeiten

The Seasons · Les Saisons

für Klavier
for Piano
pour Piano

opus 37bis

Herausgegeben von / Edited by / Éditées par
Polina Vajdman und / and / et Ljudmila Korabel'nikova

Vorwort von / Preface by / Préface de
Thomas Kohlhase

Hinweise zur Aufführung von / Notes on performance by / Indications pour l'exécution
Lev Vinocour

ED 20094
ISMN 979-0-001-14592-3

www.schott-music.com

Mainz · London · Berlin · Madrid · New York · Paris · Prague · Tokyo · Toronto
© 2007/2018 SCHOTT MUSIC GmbH & Co. KG, Mainz · Printed in Germany

Contents / Inhalt / Contenu

Vorwort

Tschaikowskys „Jahreszeiten", neben der Folge von vierundzwanzig kostbaren Klavierstücken „à la Schumann" für Kinder („Kinderalbum" op. 39) sein beliebtester Klavierzyklus, verdanken wir einer schönen Idee des Petersburger Verlegers Nikolaj Bernard. Im November 1875 bat er Tschaikowsky, für die zwölf Jahrgangsnummern 1876 seiner Zeitschrift „Nouvelliste" jahreszeitlich passende Klavierstücke zu komponieren. Tschaikowsky, gelockt durch ein hohes Honorar und „sehr in der Stimmung, mich jetzt mit Klavierstücken zu beschäftigen" (Brief an Bernard vom 24. November) schrieb die Stücke von Ende 1875 bis Mai 1876. Als vollständige Sammlung mit dem Untertitel „Zwölf charakteristische Bilder" erschienen sie ebenfalls noch 1876 bei Bernard und, neu gestochen, als „12 Morceaux caractéristiques op. 37 bis" 1885 bei Tschaikowskys Moskauer Hauptverleger P. I. Jurgenson. (Die Opuszahl 37 hat Jurgenson zweimal vergeben, zuerst 1879 an die „Grande Sonate".)

Bewusst hat sich Tschaikowsky bei der Komposition der „Jahreszeiten" auf die Erwartungen einer breiten, gebildeten und musikinteressierten Subskribentenschaft eingestellt. Dem Verleger Bernard schrieb er am 13. Dezember 1875: „Wenn Ihnen das zweite Stück untauglich erscheint [... und wenn] Sie eine Umarbeitung der «Butterwoche» [Februar: Karneval] wünschen, so genieren Sie sich bitte nicht und seien Sie überzeugt, dass ich Ihnen rechtzeitig, d. h. zum 15. Januar, ein anderes Stück schreiben werde. Sie zahlen mir einen so ungeheuren Preis, dass Sie das volle Recht haben, jede Änderung, Ergänzung, Kürzung und Neukomposition zu verlangen." Das hat Bernard, der 1873-75 schon vier einzelne Romanzen Tschaikowskys ohne Opuszahl als Beilagen zum „Nouvelliste" publiziert hatte, nicht für nötig befunden.

Bernard hatte nicht nur den Gesamttitel und die Titel der einzelnen Stücke vorgegeben, er stellte ihnen auch jeweils einige Zeilen aus Gedichten bekannter russischer Lyriker voran, die mehr oder weniger assoziativ mit den Titeln der Kompositionen harmonieren. (Diese Epigramme werden in der vorliegenden Ausgabe in der englischen Version des von Alexander Poznansky und Brett Langston herausgegebenen „The Tchaikovsky Handbook", Band 1, Bloomington & Indianapolis 2002, und in der deutschen Übertragung von Prof. Dr. Reinhard Lauer, Göttingen, mitgeteilt.) Offenbar hat Bernard die Epigramme erst nach der Komposition der Stücke ausgewählt; man darf sie also nicht als „literarische Vorlage" oder gar als „Programm" der Kompositionen verstehen. Deren charakteristische „Bilder", so hat der bekannte Musikforscher Boris Assafjew in seiner Russischen Musikgeschichte (Leningrad 1930) geschrieben, stellten „eine Poetisierung der russischen Natur und des ländlichen Alltags" dar, „betrachtet aus dem Blickwinkel des «Lebens in den Herrenhäusern»." Verleger und Illustrator der Erstausgabe scheinen dies ganz ähnlich gesehen zu haben: Die den Stücken jeweils vorangehenden Titelseiten sind mit entsprechenden genrehaften Darstellungen (Kupferstichen) ausgestattet. (Ähnliche Abbildungen gibt es übrigens in Jurgensons Originalausgaben des Kinderalbums op. 39 und der Sechzehn Kinderlieder op. 54.)

Wie reizvoll es auch scheinen mag darüber zu spekulieren, welche bildlichen oder poetischen Assoziationen die von Bernard vorgegebenen Titel beim Komponisten ausgelöst haben könnten und welche „malenden" musikalischen Äquivalente Tschaikowsky auch gefunden hat für das turbulente Volksfest in der Karnevals- bzw. „Butterwoche" (Februar), für das zwitschernde Frühlings-„Lied der Lerche" (März), die herrschaftliche „Jagd" (September) und die klingelnde „Troika"-Fahrt (November) – alle Stücke sind, ebenso wie die reizenden Miniaturen des „Kinderalbums", Charakterstücke im Schumannschen Sinne, musikalisch-poetische Stimmungsbilder und sogar, wie im Falle der „Ernte" (August), „absolute Musik" (im Autograph lautet der Haupttitel des Stückes: „Scherzo") oder, im Falle der Weihnachtsnummer, ein Tanz in Form eines eingängigen Walzers.

Zum Notentext

Der Notentext der vorliegenden Ausgabe folgt demjenigen im betreffenden Band 69a der New Čajkovskij Edition (NČE) – bis auf einige weiter unten genannte Lesarten. Besonders hingewiesen sei im Übrigen auf die Akzidentiensetzung der NČE und der vorliegenden Ausgabe, die weitgehend auf die vor allem in praktischen Ausgaben üblichen „Warnungsakzidentien" verzichten. Das heißt: Vorzeichen gelten jeweils nur für einen Takt, ein System und die jeweilige Oktavlage.

Die Originalquellen der „Jahreszeiten" sind: die autographe Druckvorlage im Staatlichen Zentralen „Glinka" – Museum für Musikkultur, Moskau (Signatur: fol. 88, No. 114; es fehlt Nr. 4, „April"); die Erstausgabe in Form der zwölf einzelnen Nummern als Beilagen zu der in St. Petersburg erscheinenden Zeitschrift „Nouvelliste", Januar bis Dezember 1876; die zwölf Nummern in einem Heft und auch einzeln, Verlag N. Bernard, St. Petersburg 1876; sowie die Ausgaben von Tschaikowskys Hauptverleger P. I. Jurgenson, Moskau 1885 (kein Exemplar nachweisbar) sowie die Neuausgaben 1890 (sie liegt der NČE als Haupttext zugrunde) und 1903 mit dem Titelzusatz „Nouvelle édition revue par l'auteur en 1891" (dieser Edition folgen zahlreiche posthume Ausgaben der „Jahreszeiten"). Die Herausgeberinnen des Bandes NČE 69a bezweifeln übrigens die Richtigkeit des Hinweises auf die Durchsicht der Neuausgabe durch den Komponisten, weil es dafür keine dokumentarische Evidenz gebe.

In den Originalquellen gibt es folgende fragliche Lesarten, bei deren Diskussion die vorliegende Ausgabe zu anderen Entscheidungen kommt als die NČE:

1) Im Autograph und in den Originalausgaben bis 1890 ist Nr. 1 („Januar") zwei Takte kürzer als in der Jurgenson-Ausgabe von 1903 („revue par l'auteur en 1891"). In ihr sind nach Takt 49 zwei Takte ergänzt; sie entsprechen den Takten 33-34 und vervollständigen die periodische Struktur entsprechend der Parallelstelle Takt 29 ff. Eine vom Komponisten beabsichtigte „Variatio" durch Verkürzung der gleichmäßigen periodischen Reihung ist sehr unwahrscheinlich; deshalb hat sich auch der Herausgeber des betreffenden Bandes 52 (Moskau und Leningrad 1948, S. 6) der alten Tschaikowsky-Gesamtausgabe entschlossen, die beiden Takte nach der Jurgenson-Ausgabe von 1903 zu ergänzen. Das erscheint musikalisch unbedingt zwingend. Und warum sollte man auch an der Richtigkeit des Titelzusatzes „revue par l'auteur en 1891" zweifeln – welchen Grund hätte der Verleger für eine falsche Behauptung?

Im Übrigen lässt sich das Fehlen der zwei Takte im Autograph leicht erklären, und zwar sozusagen arbeitstechnisch: Beim Seitenwechsel im Autograph nach Takt 46 schreibt Tschaikowsky, offenbar weil er in seiner Konzeptvorlage Takt 46 mit dem gleichlautenden Takt 48 verwechselt, sogleich Takt 49 und 50, bemerkt jedoch den falschen Anschluss unmittelbar danach, streicht die zuletzt geschriebenen beiden Takte durch und notiert den richtigen Anschlusstakt, versehentlich aber nicht als zweiten Takt des ersten, sondern des zweiten Zweitakters. (Das heißt, beim Korrigieren eines Fehlers unterläuft ihm ein neuer Fehler.) Die „verloren gegangenen" zwei Takte werden in der Jurgenson-Ausgabe von 1903 ergänzt – wie man vermuten darf, auf eine frühere Veranlassung des Komponisten. In der vorliegenden Ausgabe werden die beiden Takte ebenfalls ergänzt.

2) In Nr. 4 („April"), Takt 75, unteres System, stimmen alle Originalausgaben (das Autograph dieser Nummer ist verloren) und beide Gesamtausgaben überein: ♪♪♪ Dass Tschaikowsky in diesem Takt aber anders verfährt als in allen anderen ähnlichen Fällen der Nummer (siehe vor allem die oktavierte Wiederholung in Takt 79), ist nicht wahrscheinlich. Deshalb liest die vorliegende Ausgabe: ♪♪♪

3) In Nr. 5 („Mai") haben Autograph und Originalquellen einen Haltebogen a-a in Takt 83, nicht jedoch in Takt 16 (jeweils oberes System). Alte und neue Gesamtausgabe gleichen nun die erste Stelle an die zweite an und ergänzen einen Bogen in Takt 16. Umgekehrt wäre es musikalisch sinnvoller, also den „originalen" Bogen in Takt 83 zu streichen und in Takt 16 keinen Bogen zu ergänzen. So verfährt die vorliegende Ausgabe.

4) In Nr. 6 („Juni"), T. 74, unteres System, erstes Viertel, lesen alle Quellen sowie alte und neue Gesamtausgabe nur G. In der vorliegenden Ausgabe wird, analog Takt 23 und im Hinblick auf die diatonische fallende Skala des Vortaktes, die in den Ton g münden soll, eben dieser Ton g ergänzt.

5) Auf eine Unsicherheit bzw. Korrektur im Autograph ist die unterschiedliche Interpretation des Übergangs von der Reprise in die Coda von Nr. 12, Walzer („Weihnachten"), zurückzuführen. Im Autograph hatte Tschaikowsky die Wiederholung des Walzers zunächst mit Buchstaben und der Taktsummenzahl 87 angegeben. Dies wurde gestrichen und, offenbar von einem Verlagsmitarbeiter, aber zweifellos auf Veranlassung des Komponisten, durch eine verbale Anmerkung mit Signum am Ende des vorletzten Walzer-Takts (86) ersetzt. Das Signum zeigt hier und in den Originaldrucken bis 1903 den Übergang der Walzer-Wiederholung (Takt 1-86) in die Coda (Takt 119 ff.) an. In der alten und neuen Gesamtausgabe wird das Signum dagegen hinter den letzten Takt (87) des Walzers gesetzt. Begründet wird dieser Eingriff mit seiner musikalischen Logik und dem Hinweis auf die ursprüngliche, wenn auch gestrichene autographe Angabe zur Wiederholung der Takte 1-87. Was die musikalische „Logik" betrifft, so scheint uns der Übergang im korrigierten Autograph und in den Originaldrucken vom dominantischen Takt 86 (Es-Dur) in den verminderten Septakkord über dem Tonika-Basston As zu Beginn der Coda als unbedingt sinn- und geistvoller als die sinn- und spannungslose Wiederholung des As (Takt 87 und Beginn der Coda). Und was den Quellenbefund betrifft, muss die eindeutige Version des Übergangs im Autograph und in den zeitgenössischen Drucken von Takt 86 aus schon deshalb als authentisch angesehen werden, weil Tschaikowsky diese Ausgaben zum Druck freigegeben hat. Die vorliegende Ausgabe folgt daher den Originalquellen.

Thomas Kohlhase

Hinweise zur Aufführung

In Tschaikowskys Werken für Klavier verbinden sich, wie man das bei kaum einem anderen Komponisten findet, ein schier unglaublicher Reichtum an melodischen Einfällen mit einer essentiell gesanglichen Natur dieser Musik und der schwer wiederzugebenden scheinbaren Einfachheit des ausgebreiteten Materials. Berücksichtigt man dazu noch das Fehlen jeglicher extrovertierter virtuoser Effekte, wird ohne weiteres verständlich, warum Tschaikowskys Klavierkompositionen, etwa im Gegensatz zu seinen allgemein bekannten Ballettmusiken und symphonischen Werken, so viel weniger populär sind. Die folgenden Hinweise sollen angehenden sowie konzertierenden Pianisten möglichst anschauliche und praktische Empfehlungen geben, die vor allem den eminent vokalen Ursprung dieser Werke im Blick haben.

Voraussetzung für eine adäquate Aufführung von Tschaikowskys Klavierkompositionen ist die Beherrschung der Kunst des Singens auf dem Klavier, das heißt: des Musizierens mit vollem, schönem Klang, ausdrucksstarkem Intonieren und Phrasieren sowie feinem Differenzieren von Melodie und Begleitung – wobei letztere oft vielfältige polyphone Elemente enthält. Auch die durchweg symphonische Denkweise der musikalischen Sprache Tschaikowskys gilt es zu berücksichtigen. Die ganze Palette seiner Orchesterfarben und Klangnuancen, vom sonoren Détaché bis zum spitzen Staccato (dem Pizzicato der Streichinstrumente ähnlich) findet man auch in den vorliegenden Klavierpartituren.

Mit der Kunst des Singens auf dem Klavier ist die Kunst des sinnvollen, fein ausgearbeiteten Pedalgebrauchs untrennbar verbunden. Tschaikowsky selbst hat extrem wenige Pedalangaben in seine Manuskripte und Druckausgaben eingetragen;[1] er verlässt sich generell, wie es in einigen Klavierpartituren ausdrücklich heißt, „auf den Geschmack der Pianisten", die seine Kompositionen „der Aufführung für würdig erachten". Deshalb habe ich, unter Berücksichtigung der spieltechnischen Gegebenheiten moderner Konzertinstrumente und langjähriger Konzerterfahrung, in der vorliegenden Ausgabe die sinnvollsten Möglichkeiten des Pedalgebrauchs genau angegeben. Man beachte besonders die Verwendung des verzögerten, ununterbrochenen Pedals sowie die unterschiedlichen Positionen der Sternchen als „Auflösungszeichen".

Auch mit dem Fingersatz hat Tschaikowsky sich nur am Rande beschäftigt. Lediglich sporadisch findet man entsprechende Eintragungen in seinen Manuskripten. Für die Aufführungspraxis ist dieser Aspekt jedoch oft von entscheidender Bedeutung. Denn vollkommenes Legatospiel, melodische Kantabilität und Ausdrucksstärke der polyphonen Elemente lassen sich nur dann verwirklichen, wenn man die verschiedenen physiologischen Eigenschaften der einzelnen Finger berücksichtigt: die Kraft des Daumens, die Präzision und Leichtigkeit des kleinen Fingers, die Zärtlichkeit und Sanftheit des dritten und vierten Fingers sowie die Treffsicherheit des Zeigefingers. In der vorliegenden Ausgabe werden die wenigen originalen Fingersätze Tschaikowskys in kursiver Type, die von mir vorgeschlagenen in gerader Type gedruckt.

Um den melodischen Fluss nicht zu stören, aber auch um unnötige hektische Bewegungen in schnellem Passagenwerk zu vermeiden, habe ich manchmal die Verteilung des Materials auf die Hände, wie sie durch die Verteilung des Notentextes auf die Systeme angedeutet ist, geändert, und zwar durch die Zusätze r.H. und l.H. (rechte Hand, linke Hand) und Klammerkennzeichnung der betreffenden Töne. Diese Vorschläge sind schon deshalb gerechtfertigt, weil der Komponist selbst kein konzertierender Pianist war und einige aufführungspraktische Aspekte, die sich insbesondere auf dem Konzertpodium bemerkbar machen, außer Acht ließ.

Abschließend möchte ich allgemeine Hinweise zur Aufführung der einzelnen Stücke des „Jahreszeiten"-Zyklus geben, die auf die angemessene Darstellung ihrer Charaktere zielen.

JANUAR. Man achte auf längere horizontale Linien und lasse sich nicht durch kleinräumigere Legatozeichen zur Unterbrechung des lyrischen Flusses verführen.

FEBRUAR. Das Stück sollte kraftvoll, mit Gewicht und Bedeutung vorgetragen werden.

MÄRZ. Transparent und gefühlsmäßig zurückhaltend.

APRIL. Man achte, wie im Januar-Stück, auf die ruhige Bewegung längerer (mindestens achttaktiger) Linien.

MAI. Dieses Stück im 9/8-Takt spiele man präzise und ohne Eile. Auch das „Allegro giocoso" des Mittelteils nehme man nicht zu rasch.

JUNI. Nicht zu langsam; trotz des 4/4-Takts die für die Barkarole typische rollende Bewegung durchhalten.

JULI. Einfach, rhythmisch präzis und „im Volkston" vorzutragen.

AUGUST. Bewegt, dabei alle sechs Achtel ausspielen. Im Mittelteil das Anfangstempo nicht ändern und auf die langen melodischen Linien achten.

SEPTEMBER. Sehr rhythmisch, wie ein majestätischer Marsch.

OKTOBER. Nicht zu langsam, ohne Weinerlichkeit, einfach und liedhaft.

NOVEMBER. Aufforderung zu einer Troika-Fahrt. Elegant, ohne Eile.

DEZEMBER. Ruhiger und zärtlicher Walzer.

Lev Vinocour

---

[1] Die einzige originale Pedalangabe in den „Jahreszeiten" (Nr. 6, Takt 53) steht übrigens nicht schon im Autograph, sondern erst in den zeitgenössischen Druckausgaben von Tschaikowskys Hauptverleger P. I. Jurgenson, Moskau 1885 und 1890.

Preface

Tchaikovsky's 'Seasons' is his most popular set of piano pieces besides the Children's Album Op. 39, that series of twenty-four delightful piano pieces 'à la Schumann'. 'The Seasons' owes its existence to an idea put forward by the St Petersburg publisher Nikolai Bernard, who asked Tchaikovsky in November 1875 to compose piano pieces appropriate for each of the twelve monthly issues of his journal 'Nouvelliste' for 1876. Tchaikovsky, attracted by a substantial fee and 'very much in the mood for working on piano pieces' (letter to Bernard of 24 November), wrote the pieces between the end of 1875 and May 1876. The entire collection was published by Bernard in 1876 with the subtitle 'Twelve characteristic pictures' and again in 1885, freshly engraved, as '12 Morceaux caractéristiques Op. 37b' by Tchaikovsky's main publisher in Moscow, P. I. Jurgenson. (Jurgenson used the opus number 37 twice for Tchaikovsky's work, first allocating it to the 'Grande Sonate' in 1879.)

In composing the 'Seasons' Tchaikovsky deliberately envisaged a group of subscribers who were broadly educated and interested in music. On 13 December 1875 he wrote to the publisher Bernard: 'If you think the second piece isn't good enough [... and if] you would like me to rework the Shrovetide celebration of maslyanitsa [February: Karneval], feel free to let me know and be assured that I will write you another piece in plenty of time, i.e. by 15 January. You are paying me so handsomely that you are absolutely entitled to demand any kind of changes, additions, cuts and new composition.' Bernard, who had already published four individual Romances without opus numbers by Tchaikovsky in 1873-75 as supplements to the 'Nouvelliste', did not find it necessary to do so.

Bernard not only provided the overall title and the titles of the individual pieces; at the head of each piece he also put a few lines from poems by well-known Russian poets that might be associated in some way with the titles of the compositions. (These epigrams are included in the present edition, in the English version used in 'The Tchaikovsky Handbook' edited by Alexander Poznansky and Brett Langston, Vol. 1, Bloomington & Indianapolis 2002, and in the German version by Prof. Dr. Reinhard Lauer, Göttingen.) Bernard evidently did not choose the epigrams until after the pieces had been composed, so they are not to be regarded as 'literary models' or as providing a 'programme' for the music. Their characteristic imagery, according to the well-known music scholar Boris Assafiev in his Russian history of music (Leningrad 1930), represents 'a poetic vision of the Russian landscape and rural daily life as seen from the perspective of the gentry'. The publisher and illustrator of the first edition seem to have had a very similar vision: the title pages preceding each of the pieces are adorned with engravings of a corresponding genre. (Similar pictures also appear in Jurgenson's original editions of the Children's Album Op. 39 and Sixteen Children's Songs Op. 54.)

However tempting it may be to speculate over what images or poetic associations the titles provided by Bernard might have conjured up for the composer and what evocative musical equivalents Tchaikovsky found for the lively folk festival in the carnival celebration of Shrovetide (February), the twittering sounds of Spring in the 'Song of the lark' (March), the aristocratic 'Hunt' (September) and the jingling 'Troika' ride (November) – all these pieces, like the delightful miniatures in the 'Children's Album', are character pieces in the sense applied to Schumann: musically and poetically evocative pieces and, as in the case of the 'Harvest' (August), 'absolute music' (in the original manuscript the main title of the piece is 'Scherzo') or, in the case of the Christmas number, a dance in the form of a simple waltz.

The musical score

The score of the present edition is based upon that presented in volume 69a of the New Tchaikovsky Edition (NCE) – apart from a few details listed further below. Special attention is drawn to the use of accidentals in the NCE and the present edition, which generally refrain from using the 'reminder accidentals' frequently used in performance editions. This means that accidentals apply in each case to a single bar, one system and the octave specified.

The source documents used for 'The Seasons' are: the setting copy written out by the composer, kept in the Glinka Central State Museum for Musical Culture, Moscow (library code: fol. 88, No. 114; No. 4, 'April', is missing); the first edition in the form of twelve individual numbers published as supplements to the St Petersburg journal the 'Nouvelliste' in January to December 1876; all twelve numbers published both in a single volume and separately by N. Bernard, St. Petersburg in 1876; also editions by Tchaikovsky's main publisher P. I. Jurgenson in Moscow of 1885 (no copies have survived) and new editions of 1890 (based chiefly on the NCE) and 1903 with 'Nouvelle edition revue par l'auteur en 1891' added to the title (numerous posthumous editions of 'The Seasons' are based on this edition). The editors of the NCE volume 69a question the accuracy of reports of the composer checking through the new edition, as there is no documentary evidence for this.

In the original sources the following questionable details appear, where after discussion the present edition reaches conclusions different to the NCE:

1) In the original manuscript and in early editions up to 1890 No. 1 ('January') is two bars shorter than in Jurgenson's edition of 1903 (*'revue par l'auteur en 1891'*). Here two bars have been added after bar 49; they correspond to bars 33-34 and complete the structure of the phrase to match that in bar 29 ff. A *'Variatio'* envisaged by the composer by shortening the phrase in an evenly matched series is very unlikely; this is why the editor of the volume in question, vol. 52 (Moscow and Leningrad 1948, p. 6) of the old complete Tchaikovsky edition decided to add two bars, based on the Jurgenson edition of 1903. This seems musically convincing. And why should we doubt the accuracy of the words *'revue par l'auteur en 1891'* added to the title – what grounds would the publisher have had for a false assertion?

The omission of these two bars in the original manuscript is easy to explain, moreover, as a matter of working technique: where the manuscript score moves onto another page after bar 46 Tchaikovsky evidently confused bar 46 with bar 48, which sounds the same, and went straight on to write bars 49 and 50; then, noticing the false link immediately afterwards, he crossed out the last two bars he had written and noted down the connecting bar as intended, but in error gave it not as the second bar of the first, but as the second bar of the second two-bar phrase. (That is, in correcting one mistake he failed to notice a new mistake.) These 'missing' two bars are put into in the Jurgenson edition of 1903 – presumably as the result of an earlier request by the composer. In the present edition these two bars have also been inserted.

2) In No. 4 ('April'), bar 75, lower system, all the early editions (the original manuscript for this number has been lost) and both complete editions concur: It is unlikely that Tchaikovsky would have treated this bar differently than every other similar instance in this number (see especially the octave repetition in bar 79). The present edition therefore reads: ' ♪ ' ♪ instead of ' ♪♪ '

3) In No. 5 ('May') the original manuscript and other sources have a tied A-A in bar 83, but not in bar 16 (in the upper system in both instances). The old and new complete editions make the first instance match the second and add a tie in bar 16. It would make more musical sense, though, to delete the 'original' tie in bar 83 and not to add a tie in bar 16. This is done in the present edition.

4) In No. 6 ('June'), bar 74, lower system, first crotchet, all sources and the old and new complete editions just give a G. In the present edition, to match bar 23 and with regard to the diatonic descending scale in the preceding bar, leading onto the note G, this G has been added.

5) Differing interpretations of the transition from the reprise into the coda in No. 12, waltz ('Christmas') may be due to an ambiguous detail or correction in the original manuscript. In the original manuscript Tchaikovsky indicated the repetition of the waltz by using letters and the number 87 as the number of bars involved. This was crossed out and replaced with a comment, with *dal segno* marked at the end of the penultimate bar (86) of the waltz – evidently by a publishing assistant, but doubtless at the instigation of the composer. The *segno* that appears here and in the original impressions up to 1903 shows the transition from the repeat of the waltz (bars 1-86) into the coda (bar 119 ff.). In the old and new complete editions, however, the *segno* is placed after the last bar (87) of the waltz. This is justified by its own musical logic and with reference to the original (though subsequently deleted) instruction to repeat bars 1-87. As far as musical 'logic' is concerned, the transition in the corrected autograph manuscript and in the first editions from bar 86 in the dominant (E♭ major) into the diminished seventh chord over the tonic bass note A♭ at the beginning of the coda seems to make more sense than the pointless repetition of the A♭ (bar 87 and beginning of the coda). With regard to the authenticity of sources, the clearly marked transition in the original manuscript and editions of that period from bar 86 onwards must surely be considered authentic, not least because Tchaikovsky approved these editions for publication. The present edition is therefore based on the original documents.

Thomas Kohlhase
Translation Julia Rushworth

Advice on performance

To an extent hardly to be found in the work of any other composer, Tchaikovsky's piano works combine an incredible richness of melodic invention with an essentially vocal musical style and an apparent simplicity of content that is difficult to convey in performance. When one considers the absence of any extravert virtuoso displays, it is easy to understand why Tchaikovsky's piano compositions are so much less popular than his generally well-known ballet music and symphonic works. The following advice is offered to aspiring pianists and concert performers alike, with the intention of giving the clearest possible practical recommendations for bringing out the vocal inspiration behind these works.

Mastering the art of producing a singing tone on the piano is essential to the performance of Tchaikovsky's piano compositions. This means playing with a rich and lovely tone, expressive intonation and phrasing and fine differentiation between melodic lines and accompaniment that often contains complex polyphonic elements. It is important to understand the symphonic approach in Tchaikovsky's musical language, too. His entire palette of orchestral colours and nuanced sounds is to be found in these piano scores, from a sonorous *détaché* to a pointed *staccato* (similar to *pizzicato* as played on string instruments).

The art of producing a singing tone on the piano is inextricably linked to the sensitively controlled use of pedalling. Tchaikovsky himself put very few pedal markings in his manuscripts and published editions;[1] in general, as explicitly stated in some piano scores, he relied upon the good taste of those pianists who considered his compositions worthy of performance. In the present edition, bearing in mind the technical capabilities of modern concert instruments and drawing on many years of experience in concert performance, I have given precise indications for the best use of pedalling, using asterisks to indicate the release of the pedal.

Tchaikovsky paid only marginal attention to fingerings, as illustrated by sporadic markings in his manuscripts. In respect of performance practice, however, this aspect is often crucially important. Perfectly smooth *legato* playing, singing melodies and expressive polyphonic texture can only be brought out by working with the physiological qualities of the individual fingers: the power of the thumb, the lightness and precision of the little finger, the tender gentleness of the third and fourth fingers and the accuracy of the index finger. In this edition Tchaikovsky's few original fingerings appear in italics, while those suggested by the editor are printed in regular type.

In order not to disturb the flow of the melody, and also to avoid unnecessary commotion in rapid passages, I have sometimes changed the allocation of notes (as suggested by the way they are presented across the two systems) from one hand to the other by marking r. H. and l. H. (right hand, left hand) and using brackets around the notes in question. These suggestions can be justified by the fact that the composer was not a concert pianist himself and may not have considered some of the practical considerations that become particularly noticeable in concert performance.

Lastly I should like to give some general advice on performing individual pieces in the 'Seasons' cycle, designed to bring out the true character of each piece.

JANUARY. Be sure to play long horizontal lines and do not be tempted to interrupt the lyrical flow by *legato* markings over short phrases.

FEBRUARY. This piece should be played powerfully, with force and conviction.

MARCH. Transparent and with sensitive restraint.

APRIL. As in the January piece, be aware of the calm flow of long lines (at least eight bars long).

MAY. This piece in 9/8 should be played precisely and without hurrying. Even the 'Allegro giocoso' in the middle section should not be played too fast.

JUNE. Not too slow; despite the 4/4 time signature, keep the rolling movement of the typical barcarolle going.

JULY. Simple, rhythmically precise and in the manner of folk music.

AUGUST. Agitated and impassioned, bringing out every group of six quavers. In the middle section do not change the opening tempo and be aware of long melodic lines.

SEPTEMBER. Very rhythmical, like a majestic march.

OCTOBER. Not too slow, without self-pity, simple and songlike.

NOVEMBER. An invitation to ride on a *Troika*. Elegant, unhurried.

DECEMBER. A calm and tender waltz.

Lev Vinocour
Translation Julia Rushworth

---

[1] The only original pedal marking in 'The Seasons' (No. 6, bar 53) does not actually appear in the original manuscript; its first appearance is in printed editions of the same period by Tchaikovsky's main publisher P. I. Jurgenson, Moscow 1885 and 1890.

Préface

Outre la suite des vingt-quatre délicates pièces pour piano « à la Schumann » de « l'Album pour les enfants » op. 39, « Les Saisons » constituent l'un des cycles d'œuvres pour piano de Tchaïkovski les plus appréciés. Il doit son existence à une belle idée de l'éditeur de Saint-Pétersbourg Nikolaj Bernard qui, en novembre 1875, pria Tchaïkovski de composer des morceaux dédiés aux saisons, à paraître dans chacun des douze numéros de l'année 1876 de sa revue « Le Nouvelliste ». Tenté par les honoraires élevés, et « tout à fait disposé à me consacrer à des pièces pour piano en ce moment » (lettre à Bernard du 24 novembre), Tchaïkovski les composa entre fin 1875 et mai 1876. Elles parurent chez Bernard dès 1876 sous-titrées « Douze tableaux caractéristiques », puis en 1885, nouvellement gravées, sous le titre de « 12 Morceaux caractéristiques op. 37 bis » chez l'éditeur principal de Tchaïkovski à Moscou, P.I. Jurgenson (ce dernier utilisa le numéro d'opus 37 à deux reprises, la première fois en 1879 pour la « Grande Sonate »).

Pour composer les « Saisons », Tchaïkovski se mit volontairement au diapason des attentes d'un large public constitué de personnes éduquées et mélomanes. Le 13 décembre 1875, il écrivit à l'éditeur : « Si le deuxième morceau vous paraît inapproprié [… et si] vous souhaitez que la « semaine des crêpes » [février : Carnaval] soit remaniée, ne vous gênez-pas et soyez assuré que j'écrirai une autre pièce à temps, c'est-à-dire pour le 15 janvier. Vous me payez un prix tellement élevé que vous êtes parfaitement en droit de réclamer toute modification, addition, réduction, ou que je recommence ». Mais ayant déjà publié quatre romances de Tchaïkovski entre 1873 et 1875 en supplément au « Nouvelliste », l'éditeur ne jugea pas utile de le faire.

Bernard imposa non seulement le titre général et celui des différents morceaux, mais leur associa également quelques vers de poètes lyriques russes célèbres s'harmonisant plus ou moins avec les titres des compositions. (Cette édition présente ces épigrammes dans la version anglaise publiée par Alexander Poznansky et Brett Langston dans « The Tchaikovsky Handbook », vol. 1, Bloomington & Indianapolis 2002, et dans leur traduction allemande proposée par le Professeur Dr. Reinhard Lauer, Göttingen). Manifestement, le choix des épigrammes par Bernard est postérieur à la composition des morceaux ; elles ne peuvent donc être considérées comme source d'inspiration ni comme programme des compositions. Selon le musicologue russe Boris Assafiev dans son histoire de la musique russe (Léningrad 1930), leurs « tableaux » caractéristiques dépeignent « une poétisation de la nature russe et de la vie quotidienne à la campagne », « perçue depuis la vie dans les 'maisons de maîtres' ». L'éditeur et illustrateur de la première édition semblent avoir partagé ce point de vue : les pages de titre précédant chacune des pièces sont illustrées de scènes de genre (gravures) allant en ce sens. (Des illustrations similaires figurent d'ailleurs dans les éditions originales de l'album pour les enfants op. 39 et des seize chansons pour enfants op. 54 publiées par Jurgenson).

Il serait tentant de spéculer sur les associations visuelles ou poétiques suscitées dans l'esprit du compositeur par les titres imposés par Bernard et sur les équivalents musicaux « descriptifs » trouvés par Tchaïkovski pour illustrer l'effervescence de la fête populaire du « Carnaval » et de la semaine des crêpes (février), les gazouillis printaniers et « Le Chant de l'alouette » (mars), la merveilleuse « Chasse » (septembre) et la promenade en « Troïka » au son des clochettes (novembre). Pour autant, à l'instar des charmantes miniatures de l'album pour les enfants, toutes ces pièces sont des pièces de caractère au sens schumannien, des tableaux d'ambiance musico-poétiques, voire de la « musique absolue », comme c'est le cas de « La Moisson » (août), (dans le manuscrit autographe, le titre principal de ce morceau est « Scherzo ») ou du numéro de « Noël » qui est une danse entraînante en forme de valse.

À propos de la partition

Hormis quelques variantes indiquées ci-dessous, la partition de la présente édition repose sur celle du volume correspondant de la New Čajkovskij Edition (NČE). Nous attirons tout particulièrement l'attention sur le placement des altérations accidentelles dans la NČE et dans la présente édition qui omettent généralement les altérations « de rappel » souvent présentes dans les éditions pratiques. Cela signifie que les altérations accidentelles s'appliquent uniquement pour une mesure, un système et pour l'octave spécifiée.

Les sources originales des « Saisons » sont les suivantes : la copie à graver autographe conservée au Musée central d'État pour la culture musicale « Glinka » à Moscou (cote : fol. 88, No. 114; n° 4, « Avril » manquant) ; la première édition sous la forme de douze numéros séparés parus en supplément aux numéros de janvier à décembre 1876 de la revue « Le Nouvelliste » publiée à Saint-Pétersbourg ; les douze numéros réunis dans un recueil et également parus séparément aux éditions N. Bernard, Saint-Pétersbourg 1876 ; les éditions de l'éditeur principal de Tchaïkovski à Moscou, P.I. Jurgenson : celle de 1885 (pas d'exemplaire conservé) ainsi que les rééditions de 1890 (sur laquelle repose l'édition de la NČE) et de 1903, cette dernière titrée « Nouvelle édition revue par l'auteur en 1891 » (qui a servi de base à de nombreuses éditions posthumes ultérieures des « Saisons »). Cependant, les éditrices du volume NČE 69a doutent de la justesse de l'indication relative à la relecture de la nouvelle édition par le compositeur, car il n'en existe aucune preuve.

Les sources originales présentent quelques variantes sujettes à caution pour lesquelles notre édition arrive à des conclusions différentes de celles de la NČE. Elles sont présentées ci-dessous.

1) Dans le manuscrit autographe et les éditions originales jusqu'en 1890, le n° 1 (Janvier) comporte deux mesures de moins que l'édition de Jurgenson de 1903 (« revue par l'auteur en 1891 »). Dans cette dernière, deux mesures ont été ajoutées après la mesure 49 ; celles-ci correspondent aux mesures 33-34 et complètent la structure périodique conformément au passage parallèle mesure 29 ss. Une « variatio » intentionnelle du compositeur consistant en une réduction de la structure périodique est hautement improbable ; c'est pourquoi l'éditeur du volume 52 correspondant (Moscou et Léningrad 1948, p. 6) de l'ancienne édition complète des œuvres de Tchaïkovski a décidé d'ajouter ces deux mesures conformément à l'édition Jurgenson de 1903. Cet ajout semble impératif sur le plan musical. Par ailleurs, pourquoi douter de la sincérité du complément de titre « revue par l'auteur en 1891 » – quelle raison l'éditeur aurait-il pu avoir de mentir sur ce point ?

Par ailleurs, l'absence des deux mesures dans le manuscrit autographe est facile à expliquer du point de vue de la technique de travail : dans l'autographe, à la tourne suivant la mesure 46, Tchaïkovski enchaîne directement avec les mesures 49 et 50, manifestement parce qu'il a confondu la mesure 46 et la mesure 48 qui sont identiques. Cependant, s'en rendant compte aussitôt après, il rature les deux mesures qu'il vient d'écrire et note la mesure de transition, mais au lieu d'écrire celle correspondant à la première paire, il écrit par inadvertance celle correspondant à la seconde. (C'est-à-dire qu'en corrigeant une erreur, il en commet une seconde). Les deux mesures « perdues » ont été ajoutées dans l'édition Jurgenson de 1903 – sans doute à la demande du compositeur comme on peut le supposer. Dans la présente édition, les deux mesures concernées ont été ajoutées.

2) Dans le n° 4 (« Avril »), mesure 75 système inférieur, toutes les éditions originales et les deux éditions complètes sont unanimes (le manuscrit autographe de ce numéro a disparu) :

Il n'est pas vraisemblable que Tchaïkovski ait utilisé ici un procédé différent de celui des situations similaires se présentant dans ce numéro (voir avant tout la répétition octaviée de la mesure 79). C'est pourquoi la présente édition propose :

3) Dans le n° 5 (« Mai »), mesure 83, le manuscrit autographe et les sources originales comportent une liaison de durée *la–la* qui n'existe pas mesure 16 (à chaque fois dans le système supérieur). L'ancienne et la nouvelle édition des œuvres complètes harmonisent le premier passage par rapport au second et ajoutent une liaison mesure 16. D'un point de vue musical, il serait plus cohérent de faire l'inverse, c'est-à-dire enlever la liaison « originale » mesure 83 et ne pas en ajouter mesure 16. Ainsi procède la présente édition.

4) Dans le n° 6 (« Juin »), système inférieur, première noire, toutes les sources ainsi que l'ancienne et la nouvelle édition des œuvres complètes ne comportent qu'un *Sol*. Dans la présente édition, se référant à la mesure 23 et considérant la gamme diatonique descendante de la mesure précédente qui doit aboutir sur un *sol*, ce dernier est ajouté.

5) Les divergences d'interprétation quant à la transition entre la reprise et coda du n° 12, la valse dédiée à « Noël », sont liées à une imprécision, ou plus précisément à une correction dans le manuscrit autographe. En effet, Tchaïkovski y avait d'abord indiqué la reprise de la valse par des lettres en y ajoutant le numéro de mesure 87. Ce dernier fut rayé et remplacé par un signe de reprise à la fin de l'avant-dernière mesure de la valse (mes. 86), manifestement par un collaborateur de la maison d'édition, mais incontestablement sur indication verbale du compositeur. Dans le manuscrit et dans les éditions originales jusqu'en 1903, ce signe indique le passage de la reprise de la valse (mesures 1-86) vers la coda (mesure 119 ss.). En revanche, dans l'ancienne et dans la nouvelle édition des œuvres complètes, le signe est placé après la dernière mesure de la valse (mes. 87). Cette modification est justifiée par sa logique sur le plan musical et par rapport à l'indication initiale relative à la répétition des mesures 1 à 87, bien qu'elle ait été supprimée par la suite. Concernant la « logique » musicale, le passage de la dominante mesure 86 (*mi*^{b} majeur) à l'accord de septième diminuée au-dessus de la tonique de *la* bémol à la basse au début de la coda dans le manuscrit autographe corrigé et dans les éditions originales nous paraît bien plus riche et intéressant que la répétition plate et sans surprise du *la* bémol (mesure 87 et début de la coda). Quant à l'état des sources, la version explicite de la transition à partir de la mesure 86 dans le manuscrit autographe et dans les éditions contemporaines doit être considérée comme authentique du simple fait que Tchaïkovski a donné son accord pour l'impression de ces éditions. C'est pourquoi la présente édition se conforme aux éditions originales.

Thomas Kohlhase
Traduction Michaëla Rubi

Indications pour l'exécution

Les œuvres pour piano de Tchaïkovski allient une incroyable richesse d'invention musicale à une nature essentiellement chantante et une simplicité apparente unique des matériaux utilisés telles qu'on les rencontre rarement chez d'autres compositeurs. Si l'on considère également l'absence de tout effet virtuose extraverti, il est aisé de comprendre pourquoi les compositions pour piano de Tchaïkovski sont beaucoup moins populaires que ses célèbres musiques de ballet et ses œuvres symphoniques par exemple. Les indications ci-dessous visent à donner aux élèves pianistes ainsi qu'aux concertistes les conseils les plus clairs et les plus pratiques possibles, sans jamais perdre de vue l'origine vocale de ces œuvres.

Maîtriser l'art de faire chanter son piano est une condition préalable à une interprétation juste des œuvres pour piano de Tchaïkovski. Il s'agit d'interpréter la musique avec un son plein et beau, une intonation et un phrasé expressifs et une différenciation subtile de la mélodie et de l'accompagnement – ce dernier comprenant souvent des éléments polyphoniques variés. Il convient également de respecter la pensée symphonique du langage musical de Tchaïkovski. Toute la palette de ses couleurs et nuances orchestrales, du détaché sonore au staccato piqué (semblable au pizzicato des instruments à cordes), apparaît aussi dans les partitions de piano présentées ici.

L'art de faire chanter le piano est indissociablement lié à l'art d'utiliser les pédales avec intelligence et subtilité. Tchaïkovski lui-même n'inscrivit que très peu d'indications de pédales dans ses manuscrits et ses éditions imprimées.[1] Comme il l'écrivit expressément dans certaines de ses partitions de piano, il s'en remettait généralement « au goût des pianistes » qui considéraient ses compositions comme « dignes d'être interprétées ». C'est pourquoi, dans la présente édition, tenant compte des conditions techniques des instruments de concert modernes et m'appuyant sur une longue expérience de concertiste, j'ai détaillé les possibilités d'utilisation des pédales les plus pertinentes. Notez en particulier l'utilisation de la pédale enchaînée (décalage main-pied), ainsi que les différentes positions de la petite étoile de fin de pédale.

De même, Tchaïkovski ne s'est préoccupé que marginalement des doigtés dont la présence est plutôt sporadique dans ses manuscrits. Pourtant cet aspect est d'une importance significative du point de vue de la pratique d'interprétation. Car le legato, le lyrisme mélodique et la force expressive des éléments polyphoniques ne peuvent se concrétiser que dans le respect des différentes propriétés physiologiques des différents doigts : la force du pouce, la précision et la légèreté du petit-doigt, la délicatesse et la douceur de l'annulaire et du majeur ainsi que l'assurance de l'index. Dans la présente édition, les rares indications de doigtés originales de Tchaïkovski sont présentées en italique, celles que je propose en romain.

Afin de ne pas perturber le flux mélodique, mais aussi pour éviter des mouvements précipités inutiles dans les passages rapides, j'ai parfois modifié la répartition du matériau musical entre les deux mains telle qu'elle apparaît entre les systèmes dans la partition en ajoutant la mention m.d. ou m.g. (main droite, main gauche) et des parenthèses sur les notes concernées. Ces propositions sont justifiées, car le compositeur n'était pas un pianiste concertiste et ne tenait pas compte de certains aspects liés à l'exécution qui deviennent particulièrement apparents, notamment sur une scène de concert.

Pour terminer, je voudrais donner des indications générales relatives à l'interprétation des différents morceaux du cycle des « Saisons » et de leurs caractères respectifs.

JANVIER. Veiller aux longues lignes horizontales et à ne se pas se laisser entraîner à interrompre le flux lyrique par la présence de signes de legato plus courts.

FÉVRIER. Cette pièce sera jouée avec puissance, force et conviction.

MARS. Transparent, avec une retenue intuitive.

APRIL. Comme dans la pièce du mois de janvier, veiller à ménager de longues lignes pleines de sérénité (au moins huit mesures).

MAI. Cette pièce en 9/8 sera jouée avec précision et sans presser. De même, « l'Allegro Giocoso » de la partie centrale ne sera pas pris trop vite non plus.

JUIN. Pas trop lent ; malgré la mesure à 4/4, maintenir le balancement caractéristique de la barcarole.

JUILLET. À exécuter avec simplicité, précision rythmique et « dans un style populaire ».

AOÛT. Mouvementé, en jouant bien toutes les croches. Dans la partie centrale, ne pas modifier le tempo initial et veiller aux longues lignes mélodiques.

SEPTEMBRE. Très rythmé, comme une marche majestueuse.

OCTOBRE. Ni trop lent, ni larmoyant, simple et chantant.

NOVEMBRE. Invitation à une promenade en troïka. Élégant, sans presser.

DÉCEMBRE. Valse sereine et délicate.

Lev Vinocour
Traduction Michaëla Rubi

---

[1] Cependant, l'unique indication de pédale originale dans « Les Saisons » (n° 6, mesure 53) n'apparaît pas dès le manuscrit autographe, mais seulement à partir des éditions contemporaines publiées par l'éditeur principal de Tchaïkovski P.I. Jurgenson à Moscou en 1885 et 1890.

The Seasons

Die Jahreszeiten · Les Saisons

January. By the Fireside
Januar. Am Kamin
Janvier. Au coin du feu

A little corner of peaceful bliss
The night dressed in twilight;
The little fire is dying in the fireplace,
And the candle has burned out.

Aleksandr Pŭskin

Im Winkel stiller Freude schien
Die Nacht im Dämmer wider.
Das Feuer schwindet im Kamin,
Die Kerze brannte nieder.

Aleksandr Pŭskin

Moderato semplice ma espressivo

ČW 124

February. Shrovetide
Februar. Karneval (Butterwoche)
Février. Carnaval

At the lively Mardi Gras
Soon a large feast will overflow
Pavel Vjazemskij

Bald rauscht auf das reiche Gastmahl,
Der beschwingte Karneval.
Pavel Vjazemskij

ČW 125

L'istesso tempo

March. The Lark's Song
März. Lied der Lerche
Mars. Chant de l'alouette

The field shimmering with flowers,
The stars swirling in the heavens,
The song of the lark fills the blue abyss.
Apollon Majkov

Hoch am Himmel lichte Wellen,
Blüten auf den Feldern schwingen,
In die blauen Fernen klingen.
Apollon Majkov

ČW 126

April. The Snowdrop Flower
April. Das Schneeglöckchen
Avril. Perce-neige

The blue, pure snowdrop-flower,
And near it the last snowdrops.
The last tears over past griefs,
And first dreams of another happiness.
Apollon Majkov

Das Schneeblümchen schaut
So bläulich und weiß.
Und ringsum taut
Letzter Schnee und Eis.
Apollon Majkov

Ihr Tränen, geweint
Um vergangenes Leid,
Mit Träumen vereint
Von glücklicher Zeit.
Apollon Majkov

Allegretto con moto e un poco rubato

ČW 127

May. White Nights
Mai. Weiße Nächte
Mai. Les nuits de mai

What a night! What bliss is all about!
I thank my native north country!
From the kingdom of ice and snow,
How fresh and clean May flies in!
Afanasij Fet

Welch eine Nacht! Welch eine Lust in allem!
Mein Dank dem Heimatland bei Mitternacht!
Herausgetreten aus des Winters Wallen,
Wie frisch und rein der neue Maien lacht.
Afanasij Fet

ČW 128

June. Barcarole
Juni. Barkarole
Juin. Barcarolle

Let us go to the shore;
There the waves will kiss our legs.
With mysterious sadness
The stars will shine down on us.
Aleksej Plešceev

Komm rasch zum Ufer, die Wellen
Werden uns küssen den Fuß,
Sterne mit heimlichem Kummer
Strahlen hoch über uns.
Aleksej Plešceev

ČW 129

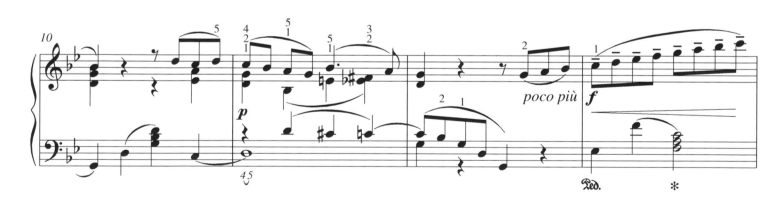

July. The Reaper's Song
Juli. Lied des Schnitters
Juillet. Chant du faucheur

Move the shoulders,
Shake the arms!
And the noon wind
Breathes in the face!
Aleksej Kol'cov

Schnitter, recke dich,
Greift, ihr Hände, aus,
Blas uns ins Gesicht,
Warmer Mittagswind!
Aleksej Kol'cov

ČW 130

Allegro moderato con moto

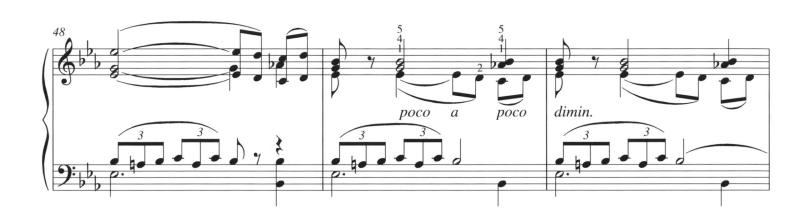

August. The Harvest (Scherzo)
August. Die Ernte (Scherzo)
Août. La moisson (Scherzo)

The harvest has grown,
People in families
Cutting the tall rye
Down to its roots!
Put together the haystacks,
Music screeching all night
From the hauling carts.

Aleksej Kol'cov

Bauern, groß und klein,
Zogen zur Mahd,
Mähen Roggen, der
Hoch im Halme steht.
Lang in Reihen sind
Garben aufgestellt,
Von den Fuhren nachts
Kreischt es wie Musik.

Aleksej Kol'cov

ČW 131

Allegro vivace

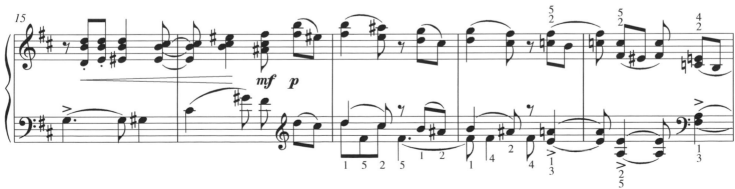

Dolce cantabile

September. The Hunt
September. Die Jagd
Septembre. La chasse

It is time! The horns are sounding!
The hunters in their hunting dress
Are mounted on their horses;
In early dawn the borzois are jumping.

Aleksandr Puškin

Heraus, heraus, das Horn erschallt;
Schon reiten in der frühen Stunde
Die muntren Treiber in den Wald,
Es springt die Koppel flinker Hunde.

Aleksandr Puškin

ČW 132

54

October. Autumn Song
Oktober. Herbstlied
Octobre. Chant d'automne

The autumn, falling on our poor orchard,
The yellow leaves are flying in the wind.
Aleksej Tolstoj

Herbst, es färbt und mausert sich unser kleiner Hag.
Blätter werden gelb, im Wind flattern sie herab.
Aleksej Tolstoj

ČW 133

Andante doloroso e molto cantabile

60

November. Troika Ride
November. Auf der Troika
Novembre. Troïka

In your loneliness do not look at the road,
And do not rush out after the troika.
Suppress at once and forever
The fear of longing in your heart.

Nikolaj Nekrasov

Schau den Weg niemals an mit Trauer,
Lauf der Troika niemals hinterdrein.
Und bezwinge im Herzen auf Dauer
Deine traurige Unrast allein.

Nikolaj Nekrasov

Allegro moderato

ČW 134

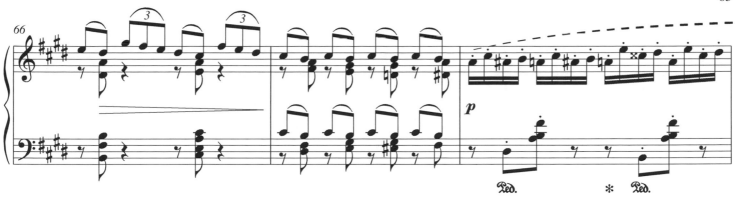

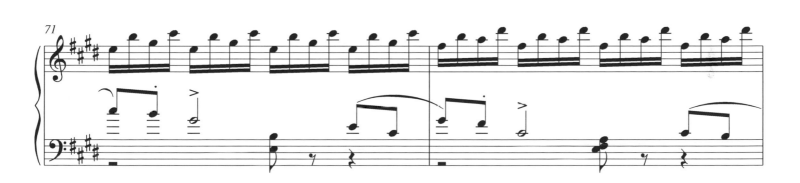

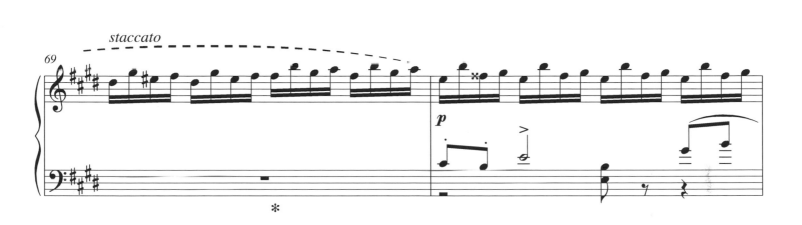

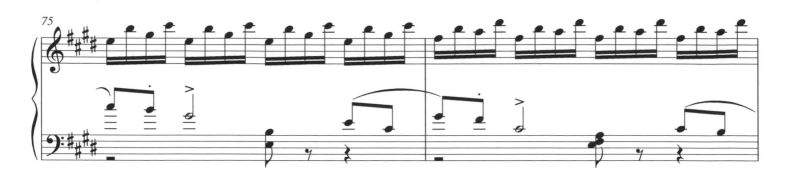

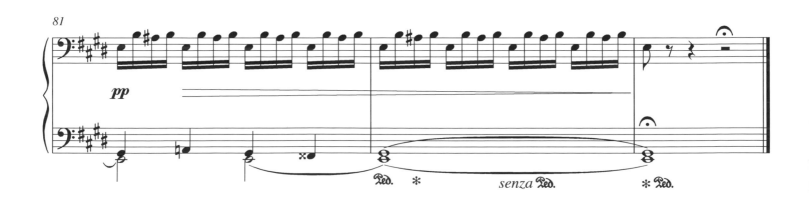

December. Christmas
Dezember. Weihnachten
Décembre. Noël

Once upon a Christmas night
The girls were telling fortunes:
Taking their slippers off their feet
And throwing them out of the gate.

Vasilij Żukovskij

Junge Mädchen sagten wahr
Am Dreikönigstage:
Ihren Schuh zur Tür hinaus
Warfen sie mit Fragen.

Vasilij Żukovskij

ČW 135

Da Capo al segno e poi Coda